The Village Of Kittery, On The Piscataqua River Separating Maine And New Hampshire.

Nubble Light, Dividing The "Short" And "Long" Sands Of York Beach.

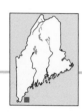

The Marginal Way, Connecting Perkins Cove And Ogunquit.

The Human Touch At Perkins Cove.

Wells, Ogunquit Beach, And Perkins Cove.

The "Bush Family" Summer Home At Walkers Point, Kennebunkport.

The Inlet At Kennebunkport.

Autumn At Kennebunkport

Cape Porpoise , Kennebunkport, And Goose Rocks Beach.

Old Orchard Beach

Portland Harbor, From Peaks Island.

Portland Head Light

The Oldport of Portland, Maine.

Maine Lobster, Fresh From The Sea At Five Islands, In The Bath - Brunswick Area.

Reid Beach State Park, Near Bath And Brunswick.

Pemaquid Lt., Indian Island Lt., And Egg Rock Light (bot)

Portlan

ead Light Nubble Lt., West Quoddy Lt., And Curtis Island Lt. (bot)

Traditional Scenes At Boothbay Harbor.

The Two Sides Of Boothbay Harbor, Connected By "The Footbridge".

Pemaquid Point Light

New Harbor, Near Pemaquid Point.

Each Summer There Are Several Windjammer Festivals And Racing Events.

Windjammers, A Familiar Sight In Summer And Fall Along Maine's Coastal Waters.

Camden Harbor, Home Of Maine's Windjamming Fleet.

Fall Colors At Camden Harbor.

Lupine, The Sedgwick-Deer Isle Bridge, And Stonington Harbor.

Sand Beach And A Cloud Covered Cadillac Mt., Acadia National Park.

A Finback Whale And Lobster Fishing Off Acadia National Park.

The Village Of Bar Harbor, Acadia National Park, And The Atlantic Ocean.

The Traditional Fishing Village Of Corea.

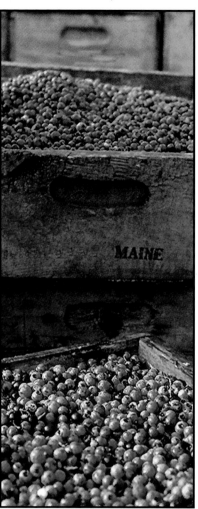

Just Caught Lobster, Bull And Calf Moose, And Maine's Wild Blueberries.

Mt. Katahdin, Top Of The Appalachian Trail In Maine.